It Is Time

Prepare Now for the Loss of a Loved One

By Errol Berk

ISBN 978-1-68517-173-5 (paperback)
ISBN 978-1-68517-175-9 (hardcover)
ISBN 978-1-68517-174-2 (digital)

Copyright © 2022 by Errol Berk

All rights reserved. No part of this publication may be reproduced, distributed, or transmitted in any form or by any means, including photocopying, recording, or other electronic or mechanical methods without the prior written permission of the publisher. For permission requests, solicit the publisher via the address below.

Christian Faith Publishing
832 Park Avenue
Meadville, PA 16335
www.christianfaithpublishing.com

Disclaimer: This is not a medical book, but rather reflections on experiences dealing with loss. The reader is referred to medical experts for any medical matters. This book is not intended to take the place of medical advice or treatment from your personal physician. Nor does it constitute psychological or counseling advice or treatment. Readers should consult their own doctor or other qualified health professionals regarding their medical or other problems. No legal advice is given or intended in this book. Neither the publisher nor the author takes any responsibility for any possible consequences to any person or persons.

Printed in the United States of America

Dedication

TO LIFE—L'CHAIM;

TO LYNDA BERK, MY LATE WIFE—
AN ANGEL IN HEAVEN;

TO MY FAMILY; and

TO BARBARA LAMARCHE FOR HER
SUPPORT AFTERWARD.

Also, gratitude is expressed to the Livingston Memorial Visiting Nurse Association and Hospice of Ventura, California, and its programs for helping to heal many people suffering from grief.

Contents

Preface 7
Introduction 9
The Nature of the Loss—Components 13
The Suggested Prescription 26
The Suggested Mandate—Discuss Now 30
Perspective and Healing 35
God and the Bible 46
You 51
Charting Your Recovery 54
Conclusion 61

Preface

This is written in the hope of helping others to successfully deal with the kind of losses that I had to endure. We all become wounded in life; what matters then is how we deal with it. Among such losses, there are approximately three million deaths per year in the United States, including an estimated one million Americans who lose their spouses. These losses entail immeasurable personal and family suffering, but such suffering can be helped. Everyone grieves somewhat differently, but there are things that one can keep in mind that could help. In addition, as baby boomers and other generations' age, there will be a greater need for this information to help heal the pain, as actuarial demographics point to increases in the incidence of grief. The following contents include the experiences, observations, and opinions of the author. The objectives include moving forward to a satisfying, healthy, and productive life.

Introduction

WE ALL ARE vulnerable. Tragedy can unexpectedly strike any family, any day, and at any time. As death is part of life, grief about that death is part of life. Your loved one can become your lost one. Whenever we love someone, or even a pet, we thereby necessarily open ourselves up to having a broken heart in the event of their loss. Developing the ties of love thereby makes us vulnerable when those ties are broken. Regularly tell your loved ones that you love them. We all are vulnerable.

This discussion has widespread application. We work to protect and preserve our lives, with insurance advisors, such as health, life, disability, liability, and other insurance products, medical advisors for sickness or injury, investment advisors, legal advisors for wills, tax, litigation, or other matters, and even automobile service advisors, but most people completely overlook what could become the most devasting loss of their lives, the loss of their closest, most intimate, most important, and most integral persons in their lives, the loss of their spouses and loved ones. The death of a spouse has been considered to be the most stressful event in life. For many, the loss of a loved one may become to some degree unexpectedly consuming—how to fix the pain. Even though you might have expected and planned for golden years together, this can be cut off, and often, the survivor may be completely unprepared to deal with the severe tragic effects of this loss on their lives. There is no going back, so what you have to do is go back beforehand. It is emotional homework to prepare for and to successfully help you through the emotional test.

As you continue to live, people around you will precede you in death. Life events can move you into uncharted, unexpected, and unpredictable developments, including loss and grief about that loss.

When this loss occurs, and grief results, the grief becomes a difficult journey, with the full array of heavy emotions—disorientation, hurt, isolation, loss, pain, sorrow, sadness, loneliness, fear, guilt, sickness, and other effects. Initially, you can be in a swirling vortex of inky darkness, with turbulent emotional forces thrusting you in multiple directions simultaneously, with the feeling of being plunged into an emotional purgatory. Flooded with tears, the feeling of raw melancholy persists. Nevertheless, with these feelings of grief, rather than let them drown you, let them move you toward another beginning.

I had a dream shortly after my wife's sudden passing. She was looking absolutely her most beautiful, in silver satins and whites, like a shimmering angel. I had said that I was ready to join her. However, in the dream, when she reached out to me, across an abyss to join her, as I began to do so, I then stopped and said to myself, I still have a life remaining.

While life will never be the same, it still can become good again even if it is good in a different way. It is important to recognize and appreciate all that you do have while trying to emerge in reconstructing an ongoing life out of what you have lost.

The journey is an effort to reestablish control of your life. Life as it had been, to some extent, has ended, and so you just have to go on from there. Initially, reflexively there is involuntary grief, swallowing up everything in its view. Then, slowly, you realize that you are not drowning, and over time, a more volitional assessment begins to awaken, slowly increasing its view of your circumstances. It eventually becomes a more decisional life as you attend to your daily condition, your physical needs of living, your mental activity, including your daily routines, your chores, your work, your associations, your remaining family, your friends, your trips, your pets, and your expanding activities. There arises up into view a new spectrum. Included in this may be an enlarging of your conversations, connections, relationships, activities, and possibly including your spiritual self, prayer, and religious affiliations. These ongoing activities begin to converge into forging a renewed self, on the path of adjustment toward a return to a sustained and healthful life.

You bring the deep darkness upward toward the light so that you can start dealing with it on a more deliberative decisional level, including your thoughts, activities, interactions, and eventually your emotions as well. While a part of your life has been lost, taken, damaged, and erased, and as an aspect of your experience and your world of closeness and communication has disappeared, still healing begins by regeneration and piecing together that lost part of your life. While things are different, you move on to adjust and refill those components. That area of the jigsaw puzzle of your life has been disassembled, disrupted, and destroyed, and there is a big hole. So you refit new pieces, one by one, into your life's picture. You fill it in with new pieces adjusted to include new circumstances, people, interactions, and focus. Perhaps also, the jigsaw picture itself has been adjusted, but you reestablish a new balance and regain control of your life with both increasing strengths and also increasing sensitivity in preserving life-long memories. Your life is like a book, and you are not yet at the end of the book; rather, you can reach out to turn the page to a new chapter and move on with your continuing life saga. The objective is to preserve the memory yet lessen the pain.

The Nature of the Loss—Components

For many, the person we lost was a large and complex combination of friend, lover, confidant, partner, helper, financial contributor, financial advisor—all intimate parts of you. As such, that lost love was an integral part of your life and had become a part of yourself. The loss of a spouse can be pronounced, and may include all these components, and sometimes may include resemblances of yourself over time, or even reflections of parents. We derive part of our own identity through our spouse. Our spouse as a lost loved one, likely was a huge part of you that had been severed off like an amputated limb, and now our remaining pathway is toward rehabilitation to regain function and to restore balance again.

The death of a spouse has been considered to be the most stressful event in life. The loss of a loved one is like a deep wound or amputation. It may seem like a tapestry ripped apart, like frayed nerves or wires torn apart, scorched and burning. Indeed, the word *widow* stems from the Latin, to divide. Similarly, its phases of recovery in grief include deep pain and gushing, eventually with a slowing of the bleeding, then early formation of wound closure, and gradual growth of healing tissue, with continued but diminishing pain, permanent scarring, and some permanent recurring pain particularly with stressful conditions yet leading to the gradual return of function with rehabilitation and engagement in ongoing life. Like a severe wound, pain is deeply felt, and healing takes time. Grief can be like a physical injury—it is sharp and painful and needs urgent response. Then, the bleeding is controlled, and proper dressings are applied. Then, the miracle of nature begins the healing process. The wound begins to close and eventually becomes calloused over, and although limited early on, function slowly returns. It is permanently scarred, but you become able to function again even with it. Indeed, scar tissue can be stronger.

Like the shock of a physical trauma that numbs the body in denial, a shock of the death of a spouse may numb the body as a denial of the severity of the loss. Such an early shock may be a natural protective mechanism to soften the full blunt of the mental, emotional, physical, and other components of loss. With our spouse, we had lived and loved, and now part of yourself has been ripped away and gone forever. The loss of a spouse leaves a huge vacuum. The more angelic they were, the more raw the world that they left behind seems to be. If there had been a large magnitude of love, there is a potential for a large magnitude of grief. Similarly, the more that the past love was a part of you, the more the suffering may be when that love was torn from you. Initial reactions sometimes include that your feelings of connectedness to reality are suddenly broken, torn apart, and turned upside down.

As the loss of a loved one in some ways is like a physical injury, the manifestations of the loss can be compared to an emotional amputation and can include feeling kicked or beaten, with pain, crying, lack of sleep, disorientation, confusion, shortness of breath, appetite shifts, a sense of unreality, a questioning of your own life, depression, and grasping for reorientation. First, the pain is raw and severe. Eventually, the healing begins. Attention to the loss, sometimes including professional attention, can be important. While there will be scarring, the goal is to restore functionality and rebuild the components of a full life.

In long-term relationships, there develops a great deal of subliminal—below the level of conscious awareness or perception—communication and accommodation over the years. This creates over time an emotional nest for each partner. Then, the loss of a partner can completely disrupt this living environment, requiring the surviving spouse to painstakingly rebuild that life. After years of mutual experiences and adjustments merging together in so many ways, when the marriage unit is torn in half, the remaining half has to learn to function without the lost half.

For some, we had it in our heads how we would spend more time together later when we had time, retire together, grow older together, and having more time together later, appreciating life, relishing relaxation, doting on grandchildren, comforting and cherishing each other, and treasuring experiences indefinitely together. Instead, with the loss of a spouse, we now are made involuntary orphans, struggling for some kind of reattachment.

When a loved one is lost, there are both immediate and long-term changes in our lives as a consequence. Your wife is not there when you come home at the end of the day. There may be no one to talk to at home, no one to share your life. There may be chores, bills, accounts, decisions, all needing attention and handling by yourself to the extent that you find your life empty. This may be a time for you to shape how you refill that emptiness.

In a deeper dimension of that adjustment, you are not the same anymore, as your life had adjusted around the life of the lost loved one, and so your life has now changed. This can be a very threatening experience for the survivor. Nevertheless, you are able to begin the reconstruction of your life and may do so now with a deeper appreciation and understanding of relationships and life's values, allowing you to develop new aspects of your life while also honoring the memory of your past. Our lives before had been figured out, had reached many balances, and had routines, processes, efficiencies, and expectations in our relationship, but suddenly these are all disrupted. This causes instability, confusion, fear, and worry. Still, we can begin to adapt and successfully come through such difficult experiences as many have done before us.

In bereavement, mourning is part of the healing process of dealing with grief. Initially, the experience can be like a free fall until the parachute begins to open. As it continues to open, our rate of descent slows and then softens to a survivable landing. At first, it seems complicated and confusing, but then you can embark upon the slow sorting out and overcoming of each of the various components of bereavement. Grief can include a wide variety of thoughts, emotions, and feelings and can include multiple factors that interplay, such as loss, love, loneliness, pain, anxiety, crying, depression, despair, denial, shock, trauma, uncertainty, fear, physical symptoms, imbalances, readjustments, sadness, insecurity, regrets, heartache, helplessness, forgetfulness, including emotional, financial, mental, and social challenges, as well as the challenge of the process of healing from these substantial elements of loss.

As everyone is different, and as the circumstances of loss are different, and as the circumstances of your lives are different, thus, the grief process for each person is in some ways different while some general concepts remain applicable. Early on, there may be periodic surges of feelings of grief, isolation, guilt, hurt, abandonment, and/or lack of purpose, and as one returns to increased functioning, feelings of grief can still wax and wane and return at times, but there will be increasing periods of normalcy. Still, it will be a different normalcy, but it will be a functional normalcy, with attributes, and a nature, and characteristics of its own.

Variables bearing upon the intensity and duration of grief include:

Nature of the relationship	Length of the relationship	Closeness of the relationship	Circumstances and nature of the accident/ illness causing the passing, e.g. sudden accident, sudden illness, long-term illness	Remaining family/ close friends

The devasting loss of a loving spouse could be represented in some respects as those emotions being symbolically represented, as it may be that:

Grief = Extent of <u>Loss</u> x Extent of feelings of <u>Guilt</u> x <u>Vulnerability</u> or fragility + <u>Depression</u> + <u>Physical</u> effects + <u>Financial</u> effects + <u>Loneliness</u> + <u>Anger</u> (some people)

or

$G = L \times G \times V + D + P + F + L + A$

In this regard, the nature of the multipliers might be considered to have a systemic overall enlargement effect, while the additurs would appear to arithmetically increase the quotient but as independent elements rather than as a function geometrically amplifying the aggregation. Notably, vulnerability can be a large factor in grief, including the sense that we are as fragile and that we are next.

An important advantage of knowing each element is that working to reduce a single element will help reduce the overall aggregate sum total. Thus, importantly, with all these components of grief, if you can lessen or diminish any one of the components of grief, then you can diminish the aggregate of grief. Thus, you can work on each component in order to decrease the overall extent of loss.

Grief

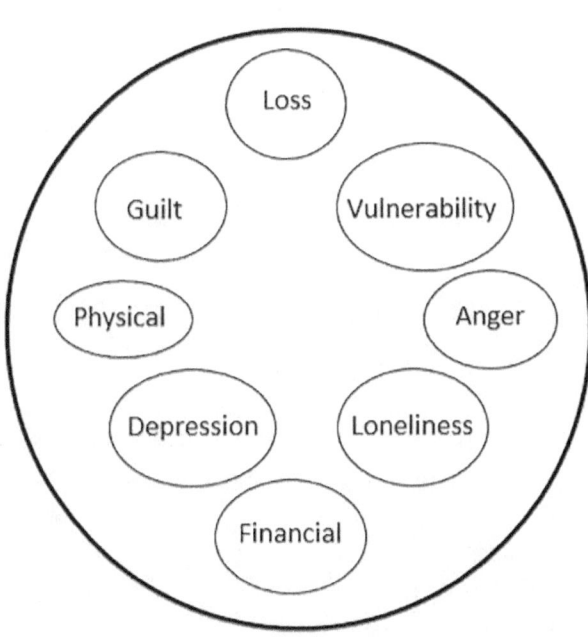

It is further noted that there may be a type of grief as to the loss sustained by the deceased, and then a type of grief as to the loss sustained by the survivor. On another level, grief could be interpreted as feelings of rejection. There may also eventually arise, even if not specifically articulated, a paradox that grief may include a component of punishing ourselves to feel bad in order to feel better. This internal inconsistency may arise by nature itself, as it eventually makes us aware, even if unconsciously, that suffering under this paradox does not make sense, and so we thereby arrive at the clear alternative that we need to move on toward real healing.

Additionally, in one sense, grief can be a reflection of a positive sign, as the other side of the coin of love, in the sense that the more the love that has been lost, the more the grief that is resulting, the greater the love that has been lost can affect other elements of grief. For example, guilt can be accentuated by the extent of love lost; the greater that love had been, the greater the feeling of guilt that may be generated as a result. But again, similarly, in both grief and guilt, the greater the love had been, the more comfort one may take that the lost loved one, because of that love, would have wanted the very best for the remaining life of the survivor.

As to the guilt element of loss, there may arise different kinds of guilt:

- Guilt over the nature of the relationship
- Guilt over an episode or episodes that occurred during the years of the relationship
- Guilt over the final accident or illness, how it occurred, and how it was handled

One aspect as to guilt has included a comparison of sudden unexpected losses to a more prolonged illness in the loss. As to each of these, the sudden shock, or the slow emotional drain, can have similar resultant aggregates of loss both quantitatively and qualitatively in the severities of grief, as six of one, a half dozen of another, but both still are amenable to healing.

Oftentimes, guilt arises from urges of wanting to save him or her, such as feelings of fault that arise in perfect hindsight that more was not done to try to prevent or intercede in the loss. It is practically uniform that people do what had appeared to be the best course at the time, and any fault now generated would be in perfect hindsight, magnified by the specter of the extent of the unexpected loss. In this regard, in suffering the loss, one might be tempted to construct pathways to suggest fault for the loss, for example, I should have driven her so she would not have been in that accident, or I should have taken her to the hospital sooner. There could be feelings of acute guilt—for the accident or illness or treatment, resulting in the loss.

As to guilt regarding the final accident or illness, perceived omissions can plague us and become magnified as we focus on how we might have saved our spouse, or prevented an accident or illness, or better cared for our spouse, or how we might regret some event or past behavior. We may have felt bombarded and tormented by what-ifs, and if onlys, and should haves, and would haves, and could haves. For example, why didn't I take him to the hospital earlier, why didn't I insist that he have that biopsy or procedure sooner, why didn't I check on him earlier, or why didn't I insist that I drive you that night. However, your responsibilities to yourself, to your loved one, and to many others is not to compound the loss but to become a better person.

There also may be guilt arising from reflecting on remembrances from the course of the relationship, including many things you think you should have done or could have done, such as times I should have done more for her, or those differences we had, or those disagreements. It is important to note that often, these are considered normal feelings arising from what you could have done as a caring person and that to not explore those feelings at some time would be unusual. Guilt may arise over what happened or did not happen during the relationship, including unresolved issues in the past. Nevertheless, if you flood yourself with what-ifs, you will never have the time or ability to do anything. All of life consists of considerations of what we could have done better, and we did what we thought was correct at the time.

As to guilt regarding the relationship, it is important to bear in mind that every relationship has periods of strength and unity but also periods of strain or friction. Every relationship has good and bad moments, and don't forget the good: the affection, appreciation, support, gratitude, struggles and projects together, activities, and closeness you shared. Periodic friction between spouses is a normal part of life, and to think back now that we should have had a relationship without some friction from time to time, or else we somehow feel guilty, is unrealistic. Every couple has disagreements of some nature at some times. The more time that two people spend together, the more it is inevitable that there arise more opportunities for differences to occur. We all make mistakes, and as we are living with our spouse, the recipient of those mistakes often was our spouse. The world is not a perfect place, and the world was not perfect before the loss. There sometimes arises a tendency to deify the ones we have lost. It might be too tempting for one to deify a lost love, which could unduly and unrealistically magnify the loss.

Some survivors after the loss go on to ask multiple medical experts about what alternatives might have better helped a loved one, and even when the experts discuss in detail that no other course would have helped or would have been realistic; nevertheless, some people find a way to blame themselves. Playing such a guessing game of guilt can delay recovery with confused speculating or beating ourselves up with Monday morning quarterbacking. Regrets can roll into guilt, which can roll into grief. Being in regret or guilt may prolong and delay the healing from grief.

Of note, if indeed you realistically could have reevaluated all of the circumstances in perfect hindsight and done something more, which usually is extremely unlikely, as you did what appeared realistic to you at the time, but if for some reason guilt continues, then make amends. Ask for forgiveness, which is central in most religions as atonement, have contrition, learn from it, and reach an enhanced comprehension and understanding of the imperfections of life. Set guilt aside, realize that the past cannot be changed, and realize that, in addition, any such thoughts can be revisited if you need to, at your choice at a later time. You also may ask your lost loved one for forgiveness, and as your feelings show that love, with such love between you, there surely follows forgiveness. Some suggest that forgiving, including yourself, may be linked to improved health, possibly being a reflection of a higher appreciation of life and growth, and helping to lower anxiety and depression. Another aspect of this, is that feelings of guilt may be interpreted as an expression of ego, which could be considered as shifting the focus of the loss onto you, as if you had the power of determinative control over life and death, which itself is unrealistic, or that somehow you are considering yourself to be powerful enough to have anticipated the situation, powerful enough to knowledgeably interpret those circumstances, and powerful enough to fix the situation so that it didn't happen. It has been considered that feelings of guilt may be more prevalent among control-type personalities as they may believe, however exaggerated, that their powers could have controlled the state of affairs, conditions, and contingencies of loss.

Do not allow yourself to be eaten up with guilt. With perspective, you can successfully find positive keys to help unlock a quarantine of guilt. Remember that what is behind guilt is caring and love, and remember that your love shows that the deceased cared for you and loved you, and would not want you to suffer in your life, and unmistakably would want the best for your life, based upon that caring love that the deceased entrusted to you and that should not be violated.

We may punish ourselves to feel bad, thinking that we either did not give, or are not giving, our lost loved one sufficient recognition. We may feel guilty for feeling okay after such a loss, and then feeling that we don't want our lost loved one to think that we are forgetting him or her. Yet our loved one would not want you to be stagnated or paralyzed due to their memory; rather, they would want you to be the best that you can be and to succeed in your life while maintaining a healthy and proper proportionality in perspective, allowing you to harmonize your functioning and your life while reconciling a setting aside of time on periodic intervals to honor their memory. While the loss may not disappear, life becomes manageable so that you can return to successful functionality. There is no reason to torture yourself, as then you lose, and your loved one, as a loved one, would lose as they would not want you to torture yourself, and others around you lose. We don't have to feel bad in order to give the departed the recognition that is deserved. It's not necessarily a letting go, but a seeing with a different lens. Perhaps somewhat like parenting, at some point, you have to decide to hold on no longer.

The degree or intensity of guilt may be, in some instances, a reflection of the intensity of your love for the lost loved one, as a rebound of your loss to you, in your reaching out for some way to protect the lost loved one. In your feeling of intense duty to protect the lost loved one, coupled with an assumed failure to do so, you may find yourself searching to justify to yourself how much you must have loved your departed spouse. Nevertheless, eventually as your life begins to heal, your need for justification becomes less acute, as you reenter the realities and concerns of continued ongoing life activities, coupled with the realization that we did the best we could under all the circumstances at the time with the information then available.

It also may seem that forces of time and the foibles of memory are distancing you from her. For example, I had envisioned that time was a vast ocean with constantly flowing currents. My loved one was on an island in the middle of the ocean, and the current of time was pulling me away, increasing the distance between us by the inexorable current of time, with powerful feelings of abandoning her, as the ocean current kept moving me away, and I was less able to see her and be near her, and I was unable to change the ocean current and return to her, and she became more and more distant and difficult to see. I also was unable to stop the fading of memory as time passed, as our memories inescapably become more attenuated.

We begin to realize that our time on earth also is limited and as such also becomes precious. So too when we die, like General Douglas MacArthur, memories of us fade away, so we must make the most of our life with the gift of life that we have, and in doing so, we can have the lost loved one live on in the memories that we sustain while we live on with our life. In a sense also, the bigger the pain, the stronger the character that eventually emerges out of that. Psychology has generally indicated that periods of sadness and crying are within the realm of normal human behavior.

Another view is that:

| The greater the guilt | + | The greater the severity of the circumstances of the loss | + | The greater the angelic goodness of the lost loved one | = | The more deeply the survivor may be affected by the loss, as the more difficult the reality appears to the survivor |

Another dynamic sometimes arises, as it may seem that a hurdle in healing is the sense that in order to heal, that is, to reassemble your life, it would mean abandoning your duty to the departed and abandoning what has been your own identity as known to yourself and to others, with a consequential sense of betrayal of their memory. In reality, however, to undermine your own progress to recovery is to undermine the gift of life that you have been given and your ability to make the most of that gift, and also to undermine their love for you, which love would have wanted the best of happiness for you, and even to undermine your ability to preserve as strongly as possible that person's memory. It is important for you to recover. If you feel guilty about being happy, remember, your remaining lifespan has potential for good times and for bad times, and if you undermine the remaining good times, then what remains in your life is the bad.

Try not to engage in daily woe-is-me emotions, but rather, as a substitute, engage in honoring the departed. You can learn to <u>balance</u>:

Moving Forward with Your Own Life	Versus	Honoring the Departed
	V	

In the pathway to recovery, be aware of two of the components and the objectives regarding these:

Pain	Versus	Memory
Decrease	V	Maintain

Considering these independently may help in proceeding with them and in separating them, as you don't want to associate remembering and honoring your loved one with pain. Of note, grief may be delayed, and then later arise, but still may be dealt with effectively.

As a caution, resist succumbing to the temptation of becoming a permanent griever—that is, don't assume the permanent identity of grief as part of your makeup, including for an identity or for attention, as this can soon sour into negative pity. If you permanently keep boo-hooing, life will pass you by eventually. Avoid being identified principally as a griever, as in being so identified that your life may become swallowed up by the death. Resist settling into loneliness. Some may ask, Is there a percentage, however small, of grief that could arise from an effort for attention, or for seeking comfort from others or for companionship? Regarding this, you don't want to prolong grief to the point of developing and assuming an identity as a mourning widow or widower, to the point where this prolonged recognition itself reaches a point of pity and itself inhibits and prevents your progress in moving toward reestablishing yourself in recovery. In order for the reverence and respect to survive for your lost loved one and for yourself, you cannot engage in a destructive course.

Grief is a formidable desert that has to be crossed by foot, but no desert goes on forever, and the other side, by definition, is no longer a desert. <u>As a large portion of grief is self-inflicted, similarly, recovery also can be effectuated by you as well.</u> Consider the positive, a wish that everyone could have had what you and your loved one had. Be grateful for the journey you had, and the time you had together, and how your loved one is part of you, in your heart, and how they made you a better person. <u>Invisible threads had bound you together, and invisible threads still bind you together. In this sense, consider that the more severe your feeling of loss, the greater were your blessings during the time you had with your lost loved one.</u>

Another element that might arise is anger, sometimes with such thoughts as: Why did the departed leave their surviving partner, why me, why did another allow this to happen this way, why did he not better provide for me, or even why did God allow this to happen? However, anger locks you into the past, and some form of forgiveness may serve to free you from the past and into a better future. Try to remember the good times, celebrations with family, births of children, school, activities, festivities, sports, travel, vacations, music, art, cars, planes, trains, and all the people you spent time with together, that is, all the good times. That is what your loved one wanted, and as your loved one, they would want that for you.

We want the love we had—but we can't have this—so we have to make a new life. It may seem as if our life were torn apart in half.

This may be seen as:
Life (old) - Loss = Grief

but then:
Grief + Recovery = Life (new)

While we cannot reverse the march of time back to the status quo ante, it becomes like having a sunken living room—it is on a different level, but it's still a living room with its own attributes. There is always hope, and grief is one of the afflictions where hope can lead to wellness.

The Suggested Prescription

IN AN EFFORT to methodically analyze and view the devastating ordeal of the loss of a loved one and to lessen its impact, there is a view toward a prescription for a remedy. Even if it can only help somewhat, or only help a few, or even if it is of only marginal benefit perhaps at first, it will be well worth the significant relief it may provide. Of note, as mentioned in the Preface, this is not a medical prescription but rather reflections on experiences dealing with loss. Medical attention is appropriate when indicated, and the reader is referred to medical experts for any medical matters.

The decision emerges to leave the pain of grief behind, and there may be the following aids to begin moving forward out of this grief.

The Suggested Prescription

In case of the loss of a loved one:

To help mitigate and diminish the inevitable mournful despair, despondency, lamentation, and grief; AND to help realistically deal with such a loss and to help lessen its effects, with a view toward helping fashion a remedy, it might be helpful to try:

#1. **NUTRITION:** Have a **balanced diet** of nutritious food with a variety of food groups and avoid overconsuming more tempting pleasure foods that often afford less nutritional value.

#2. **PHYSICAL THERAPY/EXERCISE:** Exercise, adhering to a regular daily exercise program depending upon your physical abilities, often beginning with walking, stretching, and adding aerobic exercises to toleration, usually at least twenty-five minutes a day, six days a week. Often, a gym membership and perhaps a class in exercising helps, as well as participating in physical activities or sports that you enjoy, such as Pilates, yoga, tennis, or other sports.

#3. **OCCUPATIONAL THERAPY:** Work at least half-time, that is, at least twenty hours a week. If gainful employment is not obtained or desired, then volunteer regularly at least to this degree. This keeps the body functions regular, facilitates as a diversion from the gloom of loss, and provides mental and physical stimulation for health and reorientation.

#4. **EMOTIONAL / MENTAL THERAPY:** Bereavement group support and/or counseling is often instrumental, as support groups for many are invaluable in sharing the weight of the loss, in obtaining new ideas for coping, in resocializing and realizing that you are not alone, and in rebuilding and creating a foundation in the new circumstances for yourself. Included are many books available, most of which are easy to read and have very meaningful passages to help face and meet the challenges of the loss.

#5. **SLEEP:** Be sure to obtain sufficient sleep. This also can be a beneficial consequence of following the other items in these suggestions.

#6. **STRENGTHEN TIES TO EXISTING FAMILY MEMBERS:** Consider seeking out relatives of all degrees and build and rebuild past memorable experiences by trying to reconnect with those who may be most meaningful in your life.

#7. **ACTIVELY SEEK OUT FRIENDS:** and strengthen ties to existing friends. Make time to participate in activities, which you not only enjoy but which may build new refreshing opportunities for new friends and acquaintances. Participate in those recreational activities, hobbies, clubs, and activities that you enjoy.

#8. **REGULARLY ATTEND CHURCH OR SYNAGOGUE OF YOUR CHOICE:** The time-tested historic passages, wisdom, and comfort from faith and spiritual strength often are of great support in rebuilding your life. Continue and strengthen regular ties to your church or synagogue, join at least one activity, and talk with the minister. Participate in religious activities, gatherings, and meaningful congregational affiliations. Also available are religious bereavement support groups. Remember that you have the gift of life, and the very loss you are facing demonstrates how valuable that gift is and how important it is to use that gift successfully for yourself and also for the memory that is now entrusted to your safekeeping for yourself and for others who are part of your life, as you are the steward, designee, and place-keeper to preserve the memory of your loved one as you strengthen the importance of your life.

In summary, as indicated above, physically keep healthy. Try to stay fit with activity and a nutritionally balanced diet. Health problems can compound the grief—if you feel poorly physically, it can spill over into feeling poorly emotionally. There are some bodily reactions which some think might be of assistance. For example, smiling may generate endorphins, laughing may help calm emotion and release tension, and love may support feelings of connectedness or comfort. A simple help with some tension has been to breathe deeply. It has been suggested that crying and tears may have a healing effect, possibly related to emotional responses, hormonal releasing, toxin freeing, releasing built-up tension, stress reduction, and healing.

A death rips apart a person's emotional structure. Like a physical wound, it requires time to heal, but usually over time, it does begin to heal as the raw synapses reassemble their connections and as the chemical elements recombine to become stabilized again into functionality even though it may leave some scarring.

The Suggested Mandate—Discuss Now

THE OVER FORTY years with my loved one, of course, included countless thoughtful and deep conversations. However, none of these began to comprehend the extent and depth a loss of one of us would be and how profoundly it would wound the survivor. During every relationship, by necessity, there involves some problems, friction, and disagreement. Despite any of this, sharing decades with a spouse develops profound and intricate interwoven tapestries of emotions, which grow thicker, deeper, and closer with each passing day. Your spouse has become, by necessity, a huge part of you.

These features are further brought together, combined, and coalesced by living together and include the countless subliminal and unspoken responses and interdependencies that inevitably develop over time. Even in light of any disagreement, your spouse becomes a huge part of you.

Bearing this in mind, every relationship, by necessity, carries with it the inevitability of loss. While possible, it is unlikely that the partners will pass simultaneously; the much greater probability is that one will precede the other in death. Besides the unlikelihood of a simultaneous loss of life by the two persons in a relationship, the longer and more intimate the relationship is, the greater and more serious the loss becomes.

In my opinion, it is incumbent upon the parties in a relationship to discuss between them that important aspect of a relationship, which is routinely largely ignored despite its great potential for destructive forces.

Couples retain attorneys for wills and estate planning, realtors for property transactions, investment advisors for financial decisions and retirement, accountants for tax planning, doctors for medical concerns, insurance agents for life insurance coverage and liability concerns, and even therapists for emotional concerns, but as to the really devasting and immeasurably difficult loss of losing a loved one, this often occurs when both parties have never discussed the involved emotional forces, impact, destructive potential, and lengthy sequela of such a loss and often when both parties are wholly unprepared to assess and deal with such consequences. It is through this experience with many who become engulfed in grief and turn to bereavement groups that this obvious observation is made. If this commentary assists those in some way, the effort to help those with such deep wounds will be greatly worthwhile. It therefore could be imperative that to help the hearts and love of both and the remaining life of one and the loving memory of the other, whether by accident, sudden illness, lengthy illness, or some other unexpected event, discuss <u>*now*</u> the possible loss of a loved one, <u>*ahead of time*</u>. It is likely important to act now to discuss this with your loved one, and this could be a principal key in helping with the difficult journey through grief.

The couple may need to discuss, dispassionately and with all sincerity, that the extent of such emotional loss could be, and likely will be, greater than either could ever imagine. It should be expressly and unhesitatingly confirmed by each that the surviving partner should not have whatever remains of his or her life ruined and demolished by the passing of either and that both spouses confirm that regardless of which one departs first, they express their love for the surviving spouse, and express in no uncertain terms their wish and exhortation that the surviving spouse continue on in making the very most of and achieving the fullest happiness possible in the remaining years of his or her life.

In attending many grief groups, the stories seem countless about the surviving spouse struggling deeply and endlessly in an inky darkness full of remorse, pain, regret, loneliness, and suffering. There are millions of surviving spouses in the Unites States, and with the baby-boomer generation at least currently in its seventies, these numbers likely will continue to swell. For example, in my residential area alone, of the fourteen houses along my block, six of them are the homes of widows or widowers. This small sample of over 40 percent of the homes having experienced these losses shows a huge trend for need of support, understanding, and the return to meaningful lives.

The individual consequences of people going through these struggles can be great and can also include economic losses, work losses, health care costs, mental and emotional suffering, and the waste of years of human life. The aggregated losses of productivity by so many can hardly be calculated. While some may not feel the need to engage in discussing with their spouse such a topic, the consequences of not doing this can leave the surviving spouse with years of pronounced emotional pain, substantial suffering, and significant decline. While such losses are profound, a genuine and sensitive discussion now could give the surviving spouse at lease a toehold in trying to climb out of the depths into which the surviving spouse will likely deeply and darkly plummet, and may provide a breathing-tube to allow the surviving spouse a chance to eventually reemerge and reestablish a life of some meaning in what remains of his or her days on earth.

It is also the opinion of the author that it is incumbent upon every minister, priest, and rabbi to impart upon their congregation the importance, both spiritually and emotionally, that their congregants include such a frank and loving discussion between spouses as a ministerial obligation to at least, in some way, help minister to the deep and devasting losses that routinely thereafter are inflicted upon unsuspecting couples.

It is hoped that the chapters in this book help both in the understanding of these unfathomable, wrenching losses and also in the difficult work of having to move upward in dealing with reemerging and survival in light of the heavy consequences of such losses.

It may be vital to meet with your spouse beforehand and discuss that if something happens:

#1. Don't be in pain;

#2. Move forward with your life and make the very most of the remainder of your life to be as fulfilling and happy as possible;

#3. Keep our memories of love, but don't drown in them.

We all die, and we all know that. We probably somewhere suspect that one spouse will die before the other. It is the opinion of this author that it is obligatory that a couple together spend at least twenty minutes of undistracted attention to tell each other that either you both may pass simultaneously, but that it is much more likely that one would predecease the other; and in that event, <u>the survivor is not to enter into the darkness of grief, but that "I want you to go on and live your life to the fullest and to pursue happiness; remember me, but do not suffer.</u>" This acknowledgment and confirmation could save years of painful suffering and grief.

We derive part of our own identity through our spouse. Your loved one would not want you to have a paralysis of an incarcerating memory; rather, they would want you to maintain a healthy and proper perspective and proportionality, allowing you to function in reconciling and reestablishing your life. You may need to realize now what could be in store for you, and such a discussion beforehand could be of substantial help afterward. A stitch in time saves nine. When a couple has been together for many years, although it may be felt, it also may become less frequently expressed as to what is in your heart about the love between you. In such losses, many of the survivors become aware of having taken the relationship for granted until we lose our loved one. This especially includes how you expect your partner to go on if something happens to you.

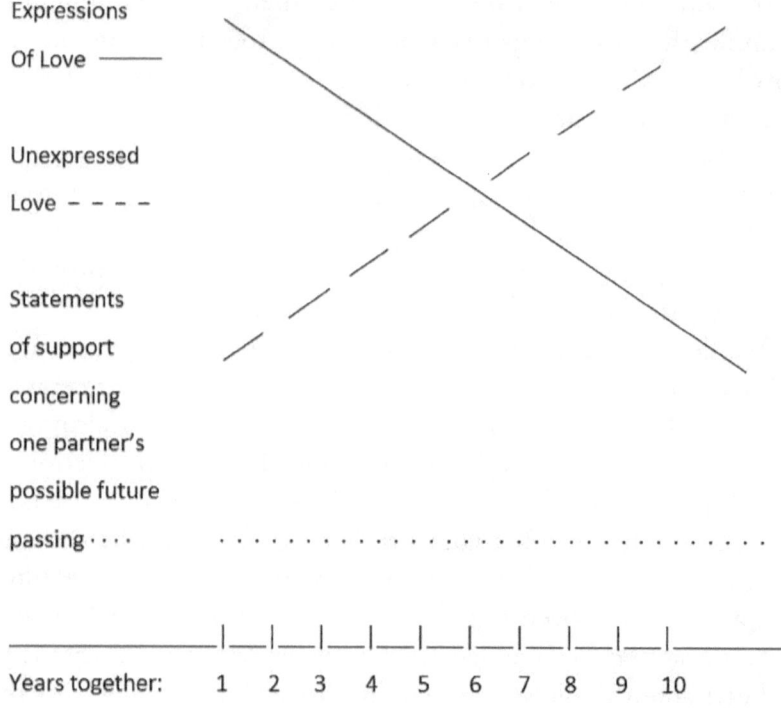

It is furthermore noted that in many instances, the loss of a love one occurs suddenly and unexpectedly, and there develops a feeling that "I wish I had just one more time to say goodbye"; however, it also has been observed that even one more time would not be enough, as more needs to communicate would develop.

Perspective and Healing

YOU DON'T JUST get over it; rather, you work through it. To the survivor suffering loss, it initially may seem that you are tumbling down into a submerged hole of inky darkness, an utter nightmare, with loss, despair, loneliness, depletion, vulnerability, and future uncertainty. Initially, it is like being tossed underwater, but when you begin to move upward and break the surface, you eventually can see <u>both</u> the ocean and the sky. You may feel for some time that you are stuck in a nightmare, but eventually coping skills develop. The grief itself occurring also could be a sign of natural healing occurring in the course of the grief process. Grief, as a process, is a journey, one foot in front of the other, one day at a time.

You must emerge from this, as is the case with every other past life challenge. You have to restart your life. We don't live on earth without experiencing in our lives certain traumas and then our dealing with them to move forward with life. With the belief, "I am going to be okay," comes the orientation to begin to figure out the reconstructing of yourself. Then, some days begin to be better. Avoid a tailspin; dying and death are parts of life and its passages.

Pain is inflicted by the circumstances, but the dealing with pain is done by us so that one becomes aware that pain may be subject to our decision-making process. Like a camera with different lenses, you can change lenses, from zooming in to enlarge every detail to having a wider perspective of seeing the broader scope of life. Your awareness of lack of peace is nature's sign telling you to now endeavor toward peace. Like traveling through a dark tunnel, first it is dark, then you see the light at the end of the tunnel, then the light becomes larger, and finally you emerge into the rays of sunlight.

Try to share feelings with those family members and friends who are receptive to having supportive conversations with you. A funeral itself is a ritual that may help in recovery in that others who care are there with you, acknowledging the value of your lost loved one's life. Sharing memories with family members may be very helpful and may help strengthen your relationships with others in the family. Some of your family members may become closer, as a sharing of the love that has been lost may, to some extent, extend itself toward other family members, with some shifting of relationships, closeness, and functions. Over time, and with conversations, there arises a sufficient reorientation or readjustment that allows you to function and to derive some enjoyment in your life.

There will always be that scar of grief, but you can return to a functioning life even with a scar. Remember, your lost loved one, by the very nature and definition of love, would want you to be happy now. To the extent you loved each other and, thus, to the extent of your loss, they would want the best for you. The worse your loss, the better was your life before the loss, and now the more important to live on to honor that love and to preserve those memories of you together. Pain also helps show that you have emotional life. Ask yourself what you can do in your living to honor them in what you are to bring honor to their life with your life, showing that they made a difference in showing how important they were to you and knowing that they would be proud of you. As an example, if your deceased wife always sent birthday cards to your grandchildren and family members, you could take that up in her honor. Another example would be to donate to her alma mater, or give to a charity in her name, or establish a memorial or scholarship.

Where the pain, ache, hurt, and grief is greater, the greater the good times had been, so you are very fortunate indeed to have lived those good times and now to have those memories as part of your continued life. Nobody can take the wonderful memories away from you except yourself. Remember the joys; if you fixate on the negatives, you can't move ahead. Like teamwork, take the baton from your departed, as they would want that, and carry on with their values, work, and memories. In a significant way, your loved one really has not passed, as long as we are there to remember them. The person lost will continue to live on, only if you live on to keep their ennobling memory alive. While death ends a life, the relationship does not end. Remember, now being apart does not mean that your loved one is forgotten, unloved, unremembered, uncherished, or disloyal. Allow the memories to be constructive rather than destructive. Like going on a trip—your visit to that beautiful place was wonderful, but your trip finally ended, and you had to move on—you can still remember that happy time forever in your heart. Appreciate the uplifting sweetness of the inspirational memories.

At some stage, you may feel that you are caught in a gristmill between two opposing, antipodal, forces:

> The desire to honor, remember, respect, not betray, and resurrect the deceased's memory, the person with whom we spent so many years with mutual experiences and adjustments, merging together in so many ways, as our life was part of their life, and so it seems like we are abandoning our own life;

> While simultaneously moving forward in recreating a new life.

The tension initially is harrowing, and then, after being battered by the crosscurrents of grief, these two forces reach an accommodation, a balance, a homeostasis, as impelled by the forces of time sorting out these things.

Our body affords us the capacity to heal. To do otherwise makes your life a futility—like incessantly kicking a tree, you'll have a bruised and bloody foot. The more you do so, the more you bruise, bleed, and injure yourself and increase the loss to yourself and to everyone else. You may think that you are doing them a favor, but who is going to keep their memory alive? Do not inflict the pain and grief you feel onto others in futile acts to yourself.

In grieving, the grief process itself is a journey toward healing, and the grief itself may be seen as a normal and healthy response in the healing process. So, in one sense, it's okay not to feel okay during the grieving process itself; and in the same sense, during the grieving process, it's a normal thing not to feel normal during that period of time. The grief may never completely go away, but it becomes softer over time, and the brutality of reality eventually becomes a memory of beauty. In this regard, it may be helpful to consider the concept of compartmentalization, to put these recollections in a special place in your mind, as the more meaningful they are, the more lasting they will be, to be disassociated, stored, and visited upon when you decide while in the meantime, you can go about living on with the life you now have. Get ahead of this—like everything else in life—move yourself forward and not dwell on the negative, which could serve to bring us down rather than forward into the meaningful and regenerative life ahead of us.

<u>You</u> have a <u>choice</u>:

The light—a fulfilling life of perspective, meaning, and contribution
or
The dark—sadness, negativity, and degeneration

The choice is obvious.

It would be wasteful to squander the time you have left. We realize that we are all vulnerable. The time remaining in your life may be thought of like a deck of cards. Even though much of the deck might already have been played, you have the remaining cards, and if you continue to play them as grief instead of life, it depletes those cards that you have left for your remaining future. The ineluctable and continuous march of time depletes our lives soon enough anyway. When age catches up to you, and others pass, you realize how precious it is to sustain your life. Life always continuously presents all sorts of challenges, and with each day, there is no end to the difficulties, obstacles, or barriers we meet; but you always, in some way, press forward. It is being fearful that teaches the importance of courage.

In intense or prolonged grief, you can exhaust yourself and your reserves and reach a state of grief fatigue. There is a fatigue factor, as at some point, you may become worn out and tired of crying. At this point, you can look around and begin to reassemble your life's many facets in order to move forward and live onward. Self-preservation may emerge as a natural engine that, by necessity, hydraulically displaces at least some of the grief. Grieving can wear out a person, and when grief fatigue begins to set in, this is a natural sign telling us that we have to begin moving on, in a new direction of healing. Eventually, you come to realize that you don't have limitless energy, and that you don't have that much time left in your own life. If emotional fatigue sets in, then adequate physical activity, proper diet, and rest play a role in recovery.

You had the past, and now you have the new life, and you learn to live with both. You develop a deeper perspective on all life. You cannot change the past, but you can shape your future if you look forward and not fixate on the past. Consider a car's front windshield being ten times bigger than the rearview mirror. Look forward and don't dwell on where you've already been. Also, a rearview mirror is there to periodically check on the past while traveling forward. In reflection, a life itself may seem like a family vacation in that it may feel like it's over before you know it. The years will still fly by anyway, usually much sooner than we know, expect, or wish.

Paradoxically, one reflection is that the extent that you miss your loved one can equal the extent you are really grateful for the time you had together. It may be that many people could only wish that they had what you had. For many, rather than getting over it, you get through it. In that respect, ask yourself, Do we honor their memory more if we suffer, or rather, if we move forward with positive memories? While we may have a desire to sacrifice for our lost love, like everything else, there is a natural limit, when selflessness becomes selfishness. Love isn't tearing your heart out; rather, it's warming the heart with remembering nurtured by gentleness and honor. It doesn't do anyone any good to beat yourself up regarding this.

As to the relative roles of potential resources, a bereavement counselor and/or group may offer considerable help, especially in the early acute stages. Also, meeting with clergy may help. Hospices may offer services for people needing to talk to someone. Just as the attorney, accountant, realtor, and doctor all have respective functions; similarly, clergy and counselors can offer personal help. Bereavement groups or bereavement counselors can be vital, especially early on, like seeking medical help early in dealing with a physical injury or illness. A bereavement group can help you move forward and reconstruct a new balance for your life. Just being present in a support group is a sign of beginning to understand and deal with the process as a comfort to help you in your recovery. There, you can share loss, sorrow, memories, hope, and recovery. You will not be alone in your suffering, and together you can find strength to move forward with your life. In bereavement groups, others have been where you are and have found ways to move forward. You can witness the progress of others, you can share your struggles, and they can help you to progress. In a group, sometimes you can feel the support of everyone's heart, and such a soothing shared common empathy can be productive of growth. Empathy, compassion, caring, and concern toward others and then also toward yourself can be mutually learned together. Just to begin healing proves that healing is occurring. As a note of caution, be careful about not being overly vulnerable; and another consideration arises in that at some point (possibly for some people, after eight to twelve months of a bereavement group), you may reach a tipping point, where you have improved to the stage that a bereavement group may begin to move you backward into a re-immersion of pain from which you already have advanced, by the rehashing early challenges of grief from which you are trying to move away.

In this regard, being alone can cause one to excessively turn inward—ingrown, negative, and limited in scope, rather than currently interacting with life. When you're alone, it's tough because there may be no other focus. To socialize may become cardinal or constitutive, and generally, one wants to avoid slipping downward into a darker abyss of isolation and solitary living. Just as there are always other people, there are always opportunities to meet new people and to establish new relationships, as you have new choices you can exercise. Sometimes, companionship can help take some focus from grief and move it forward toward positive relationships. Eventually, you may become more appreciative of life. There likely will be people who like the person you become.

As another consideration, if you are inclined, some write a journal or a diary about thoughts of, or poems to, or lists of special moments with, or special talents of, or other experiences with, your lost loved one. Some write down things in letter form to the departed loved one, with those things you wanted to say but were not able to say. Some write down happy thoughts and collect them. Some wear a locket, or wear one of her rings on a necklace, or place a photograph or photographs in a special place at home, or frame photographs, keepsakes, and mementos. Some take up painting, music, or quilting, including making a quilt of some special clothes of your lost loved one. For some, writing a letter, writing notes, or keeping a notebook of happy memories, activities, or events, or creating a memory book of photographs can help through difficult periods.

Further considerations include continuing your work, considering a new career, or doing volunteer work. The workplace can be a sort of refuge from grief. Some join a service club or civic organization. All of these enable you to think about something else, have regularity in socializing, have a schedule for participation, and have a healthy contributing distraction of doing good for the community and helping others less fortunate with the happiness and fulfillment derived from that. This includes reinforcement of how you are still a special useful human being, all of which also leaves fewer hours to be affected by grief. Additionally, pets may be helpful and supportive. Indeed, they offer a good example. For instance, we had a Labrador Retriever which had developed cancer in a leg, that was eventually amputated, and the dog immediately went on adapting, walking, running, playing, and loving, with only a minimal indication of any concern about limiting itself.

Over time, with your emerging out of the sadness, there begins a functioning, with memories which can evolve from painful to meaningful. There are natural forces at work. Included among these is a natural erosion of memories. This could be considered, in part, a healing force in the perspective of your building a new life. There is a natural movement of time forward and away from the past. In some cases, it might help to put together photographs of happy times, which may help in not punishing yourself with any thoughts that you somehow did not do enough to show abundant kindness and love to the departed. Nevertheless, try not to let past circumstances dictate how you live the remainder of your life as you seek to free yourself from the rawness of grief, and in its place, decide to obligate yourself to honoring the memories of the departed.

Also remember that focusing on the event of their passing distracts your attention from all the good and good times of their lives and their relationship with you and relegates your memory to their darker illness or accident, which can discolor what actually was the greater period and greater good of their lives. Try not to let their final illness or accident dictate how they are remembered. Rather, that person likely would want to be remembered for all their goodness and your good times together. You can see that the strength of the love proves that you had goodness and good times, for if they had been bad times, then the loss would not be felt so greatly by you. Thus, as there had been so much goodness, therefore have those good memories now and be positive about them for a positive recovery.

When reflecting on the past, try to consider that reflecting to constitute a moment to nourish and foster your recovery rather than as a time of encapsulating yourself in an enveloping preoccupation with the past or a feeling sorry for yourself. Although initially, you may be lost in a fog of grief, normally, it is not productive to wallow in grief. Feeling sorry for yourself is natural to some extent, but then summon up the strength to not let it overrun your life. In this regard, sometimes sympathy has a potential to become addictive, which could thereby hamper recovery. Similarly, be careful not to seek sympathy/attention even if subconsciously as an unidentified or enigmatic force. Usually, one cannot successfully build a life on sympathy, as it offers no solid foundation and also could pose a potential to move from sympathy to pity. Rather than indulging in preoccupying yourself with the loss, try to be busy with other things currently in life, with their own concerns and challenges, in order to shift your focus toward healing. It may be too easy to lose yourself in pain, but the lost loved one would not have wanted this for you and likely would tell you not to be upset and that there is much to do with your remaining time here.

To the extent that your love was strong, the loss is great, but so is the fact that your loved one, having loved you, would have wanted you to be happy and to choose happiness—it is what your loved one would have wanted for you, and to honor them is for you to find happiness. Use what you, thus, learned from your loved one. You can further honor them by similarly being an example of making others feel genuine love. Your departed loved one would not want pain for the living spouse so loved. Your departed loved one likely would have expressed natural charitable instincts, that would want us to have some happiness, and they likely would say, "Cheer up," and "Live life."

We have to come to the realization that we can't have our prior life the way it was anymore, and so we have to move on, and we have a chance now to create a new direction. In this regard, seeking happiness is a daily choice—do you want to be sad, or do you want to feel better and pursue and find happiness? You can learn to best nurture your heart by using your head. It takes some work to reach recovery so that grief won't eat you up; work to climb out of there to effectively deal with the grief and live life again. Push up or be pulled down. Move yourself upward, from one level to the next. Grief may feel like an ocean storm, so all we can do is learn to swim. Even surfers must conquer the challenging waves in order to reach the point where they can succeed, and then they ride back, supported and propelled by those waves. Some further analogies may be of help. In some ways, a lifetime may be compared to a train ride, with people on and off, and so experience the ride for the whole trip. Another comparison is that your ship has not completed its journey. Also, you don't become discouraged when a trip comes to an end; you think of the good times you already had, and you move on with life.

Decidedly direct yourself to daily tasks, to make it through the day, and compartmentalize the negative while you address daily tasks, keeping busy attending to more constructive activities. In order to move forward with <u>your life,</u> you can develop a healthy channeling, direction, allocation, categorization, and compartmentalization as a relief valve of the constant pressure of recurring memory. Eventually, better intervals will emerge during the day, and over time, you likely won't hurt as much, and you won't cry as much, and while life may not be excellent, it becomes good. Correspondingly, the deeper plunging into darker levels of reflective memory and grief will occur with less frequency. Do you want to be miserable, or do you want to successfully cope? To an extent, your fulfillment in life is a matter of your own choice. Don't forget that we have so much for which we should be extremely grateful.

There are difficult days, and we resist change, the unexpected, the different, and the unfamiliar; but we can change, and we can grow. Your life will not be the same, but different does not necessarily always mean worse, and with time and endeavor, you can find light, and so you just have to keep going and make the very best of your life. As in nature, there are low tides but also high tides, but usually the pain eventually will soften. Rebuilding, even without some of the past routines and rituals, develops new routines and rituals. Of note, you may think that your life before this loss was carefree, but like deifying your lost love, idealizing your prior life without its actual troubles, trials, and tribulations may be just as unrealistic.

Usually, you are better off to avoid making decisions too soon regarding your job, residence, and loved one's belongings. Everyone's pace on such factors may be different. Interacting with the decedent's possessions can be difficult, especially soon after the loss, but usually becomes less difficult over time. These possessions could include special papers, photographs, books, jewelry, clothing, and other belongings. Some, as an example, consider initially keeping one-third, giving away one-third, and discarding one-third. As to the portion kept, organize some boxes of their most meaningful and precious possessions. As to the portion given away, consider the children and grandchildren, other relatives, charities such as Salvation Army or Goodwill, or others in the occupation of the deceased loved one. For some, separating from the decedent's possessions might be helpful insofar as possibly freeing that person in rebuilding a new life. It also is noted that some life insurance policies might request a full death certificate, including the coroner's input, which could take some time depending upon a county's procedures.

Your departed loved one would not want you to have pain. So pain would be detrimental, both to the wishes of your loved one and to you. Some feel that your departed love one continues to love you, and knows what you are going through, and wants you to heal with a new life, reaching a functional level in thoughts, feelings, activities, and relationships. You will never forget your departed spouse. As the death passes, begin turning to memories of their life rather than turning to memories of their death. As she was part of you, live on so that she can live on as part of you. As your beloved spouse was a part of you, the things you do now, such as helping others, includes a reflection of, and a credit to, your lost loved one. When you give of yourself, you are also giving of him/her, thereby when you make a positive difference in people's lives, so is your departed spouse with you in making those contributions. Thus, your spouse lives on in the good works that you continue to do, and those good works also honor them. The hope is that in the future, you will say their name and be able to smile with love. Keep the good and keep their memory alive—if you do, they will never leave you and will stay with you always. You can have them to visit whenever you wish, because they live in your memories. Some beautiful things have an eternal presence—even when you can't see the stars, you know they are there and will never go away. The loss of your loved one cannot remove the triumph of their life. Live and maintain the memory of your loved one.

God and the Bible

IMPORTANTLY, IN THE Book of Ruth, Ruth loses her first husband, Mahlon; she then moved to the Holy Land, was consoled in her grief by Naomi, and Ruth commenced to rebuild her life. Ruth went on to marry again, to Boaz, and thereby so great was her reconstructing of her life that her descendants were both King David and Jesus. Thus, The Book of Ruth, this four-page book of the Bible immediately following The Book of Judges, directly portrays the suffering of the severe loss of losing a spouse, and then rebuilding your life with faith in the Lord, and becoming an eternal monument to recovery and redemption, becoming one of the most prominent world historic figures in the history of civilization. *Ruth*, Hebrew for "companion," became a world historic figure because of the things she did in moving forward with her life after the death of her first beloved spouse. Think of what it became and what it meant to go on with life and not to be swallowed up by the past.

It may be presumptuous of us to think that we know why your loss occurred. Who are we to be so presumptuous to know God's plan? Proverbs 3:5 says, "Trust in the Lord, with all thine heart; and lean not unto thine own understanding."

It helps us to seek guidance and solace in the Bible. It is by the urgency of our limited time on earth that we seek to heal and to live a full life. Proverbs 3:1–2 says, "Let thine heart keep my commandments; for length of days, and long life, and peace, shall they add to thee."

It becomes important to realize that each of us is finite. Each of us is part of God but is not all of God. We can never be God, but we can do our best with the gift of life that He has given us. We have our gift of life from God, but we're not God, and we can't be God to know all the whys and wherefores, but we can do our best with the gift of life that God has given us. Who are we to judge the unanticipated and unpredictable vicissitudes inherent in the complexities of life? Death occurs inevitably. Blame has been debated in countless circumstances, but as life creates, life can also take, both without fault. Our life's mission is to move forward with that precious gift that we still have. Don't you see, that you have been given a second chance, and in return for that gift we must make the very best of it, and not waste that precious gift of life on despair.

In that regard, every such loss is eternal and infinite, but our own abilities are limited, which already limits our ability to fully understand the loss no matter how hard we try. This underscores that the best we can do is to put the loss into perspective alongside our own limited life and capacities and to do our best to make the most of what we have been given, the gift of life. It may be difficult for us to accept the realization that we are limited in our ability to change the past, but we still have the ability to improve the future. As has been said, our life is a gift from God, and what we make of it is our gift back.

In Psalms 68:19, it says, "Blessed be the Lord who daily loadeth us with benefits." In Psalms 92:1, it reads, "It is a good thing to give thanks unto the Lord, and to sing praises unto thy name, O most High." In Psalms 30:5,10–11, it states, "Weeping may endure for a night, but joy cometh in the morning…Hear, O Lord, and have mercy upon me: Lord be thou my helper…thou has put off my sackcloth, and girded me with gladness."

The greater the loss, the greater the thing is that we have lost, that is, life, and so the greater is the importance that you live life to the fullest to make the most of the blessing of the gift of life.

We are left with a gift—a realization of how precious the gift of life is, and how we are to make the best of the gift you have received and not waste it, in honoring the giver of the gift of life, God. You can unintentionally devalue the gift of life by dwelling on the past, rather than living life to its fullest. Are we showing reverential consideration of God if we become disheartened insofar as we may not then be bearing in mind all of the incredible and inestimable beauty of His countless gifts to us.

We come to realize that the world is not a perfect place and that our participation in it can make it a better place. One must summon the courage and resolve to move forward and not to artificially incapacitate yourself from a full life, which would include memories but also include happiness. While there is no statute of limitations on grief, developing a perspective brings one back to the fullness that life has to offer. Each moment of life is a precious gift to be cherished with; thanks to God for the gift of life.

The great makeweight is the gift of life. Seek the <u>balance</u> of perspective:

<u>   Grief   Versus   The Gift of Life   </u>

Religiously, obituaries regularly include such statements as "God called him home, she returned to God, he is meeting with the Lord again, she was called by the Lord, he was called to heaven, she entered heavenly paradise, he has gone to heaven, she is happy now in heaven, he completed his mission on earth, and she went to be with her Lord." You will see your spouse again. We all go the way of all flesh soon enough anyway.

Faith may offer help. For many people, God is there for you in difficult moments. It has been considered that when you remember God, God remembers you. It is widely believed that God can cleanse with forgiveness and, with repentance, light our way in the darkness, as God is there to help all of us. In His love, we find the strength to live, and the strengthening angels of the Lord may be found in the Bible. Additionally, like Job, or like the Resurrection, or like the Phoenix, the seed of your grief may become the root of new growth in your life. Inscribe your name in the Book of Life.

Time can be an excruciating and painful factor as we necessarily have new experiences while our lost loved one has been fastened only to past experiences, further and further behind us. Like an ocean current, we are being pulled away from our lost loved one with each daily activity occurring without that person any longer. Additionally, our memories necessarily become more distant. All of these factors serve to distance ourselves from our lost loved one.

These ineluctable dynamics also serve to bring us forward to necessarily refocus on the present. We necessarily have to move on and develop a new focal point of perspective, a new normal. These dynamics also help us, however difficult and painful, to redevelop our life around its new circumstances. No matter how stressed we are, remember how blessed we are. Remember, since our lost loved one was loved by us, our lost loved one was good, and because they were good, they would want to be good to you, and since they were good, they would not want us to suffer, and because they were good, they are in heaven.

Regarding the nature of the past loss and possible guilt about it, we can't know everything, and we can't predict everything. It may be considered too presumptuous, or egotistic, or narcissistic to think that you were the operative cause of loss. In your life, as it has been going along its train track, God uncoupled a car and sent it to another track, but you are still moving ahead on the rails to go forward with your life.

One of the abundant gifts of religion includes its mechanisms for forgiveness, such as confession, Yom Kippur, and prayer. Prayer can be a form of sending love. For some, there may be a feeling of guilt that arises from the sense of duty to not forget or to not depart from your loved one who has been lost. Some help arises from traditions such as Yahrzeit, or year-time, in which there is a permanent yearly ceremony as an appointment to remember the lost loved one. This could be felt as a reassurance that you are doing the right thing. This observance is sometimes further established by a memorial plaque, which is recognized yearly on the date of passing. This can help as an outlet for those feelings, allowing us to assign those feelings to an established, regular, and reliable observance, which helps us fulfill a feeling of obligation, and commensurately in the meantime helps to free us to move on to other directions and activities while being sure to preserve your wish to remember the lost loved one. Also, visits to a gravesite or some memorial place of remembrance similarly can help with the untethering of being caught in the despair of being locked in a frozen feeling of choking obligation. If you tear your sweater—you can sew it, and although it is not the same and is scarred, it is functional and still useful.

The Yahrzeit yearly remembrance lets you know that you won't be forgetting that person, and you can reassure yourself that you continue to do right by your lost loved one. The yearly Yahrzeit candle lighting prayer includes, I reverently recall, the moments we shared together, and time cannot efface the measure of our memories. Similarly, regular prayers can help you show your continued love and devotion to their memory. God gave you a new assignment: live for your lost loved one. Another helpful activity is to write other family members, such as birthday cards, forming a bedrock of remembrance for everyone.

Also, of note, the Mourner's Kaddish, meaning holy and sanctified, has been the prayer recited for a relative in services by mourners, is over a thousand years old, as we are not the first to struggle with these personal challenges. In its designating a time for expression of loss, it thereby provides that this particular time, by being so designated, will not be all of the time. Importantly, the Kaddish focuses on two areas: one, thanking God for all His blessing of life, and two, may we all find peace on earth. This emphasizes the blessings and gifts we all have and supports a positive recovery to find peace in our remaining lives, all while honoring our lost loved ones.

You

During the process of moving through grief, when you return to the realization that you are a unique individual with the special gifts of life and special gifts all your own, you can develop the strength to realize that your life has a unique meaning and a unique destiny with remaining potentials to develop yourself for good. To a large degree happiness is a decision you make for yourself. In this regard, allow yourself to choose to be happy and to not allow your happiness to be totally dependent on what's outside of you. Happiness in life is a choice, and <u>now</u> is the time you own.

You want your reaction to matter to your lost love, to yourself, and to others, and you feel the pain as a result; but in recovery, you cannot allow that pain to incapacitate you and your life. In this regard, there may be feelings that in order to demonstrate to others the extent of your love, there must be self-denial or suffering, but in recovery you cannot allow this to incapacitate you by a loss of a fully functional life. You don't want to incapacitate yourself from being a happy person. You see, you have been given a second chance, and so don't squander that rare gift of the miracle of life on wasteful unhappiness. Our job is to move on and make the most of life with what we do have. You may sometimes think that somehow fate determined your sadness; but consider, it is you who now determines you own fate. You can control your thoughts instead of thoughts controlling you.

Furthermore, there is an additional dimension to this being that you are left as the guardian, director, administrator, curator, keeper, and steward to preserve your spouse's memory. Thus, as the recovery continues, you become able to separate the two—preserve the memory without preserving the grief. You don't forget the past memories, as you have to live on to preserve those memories, as you become a living trustee of maintaining their memories and their values, to yourself, to family members, and to others.

This can be done by learning to accept yourself and your worth, which already has been proven as your departed loved one had loved you for your self-worth, with all the gifts that you have. When you feel good about yourself, you can move on with your life. The related concept of forgiveness can lead one out of darkness. Without forgiveness, even forgiving yourself, you become a prisoner of the past. From all of this experience, you can become a more compassionate and understanding person.

It can be important not to overindulge yourself in dwelling on the loss at the expense of sustaining a productive life for yourself. There is at issue a conservation of energy and of all your available resources, as opposed to an over-expenditure of yourself into dwelling on the past. This can be considered an expense, draining away your limited life and limited resources of your future. Life is too short as it is to dissipate your energy and the remainder of your life. You don't want to throw your life away with negative time and energy in grieving. Ironically, the greater the loss, and the worse you feel, that demonstrates the more valuable life is, underscoring how valuable it is to make the most out of our own gift of life, and not to de-value yourself. You develop the capacity to allow the loss to reside within you while still learning to move forward with life and new endeavors. To some extent, you have a new *tabula rasa*, or empty page (erased slate) to fill, and you also have a new *carte blanche*, or free hand (blank paper), and to do so as your *raison d'etre* (reason for being).

A concern is that you never return to normal, as that prior normal is gone, and you have to put together a new normal. However, you now can make new plans, do new things, meet new people, and make new adjustments. You may reconstruct yourself in a new context. No one can overstate the preciousness of life, and to the extent the lost loved one was precious, you have a precious life worth preserving and worth living to the fullest. You can grow and establish an extra compartment, a shrine in your psyche, to always house and cradle the memory of your lost loved one, while simultaneously allowing the rest of you to proceed forward with your life.

In balancing emotional stress versus the pathway to recovery, you clearly have the ability to adjust. Summon up your strength, and your head will become equally as strong as your heart. Examine the situation, process the situation, and proceed forward. You will forge your pathway through the experience of grief and move from internal preoccupation to external perspective in proceeding forward out of the past. Don't overlook your strengths, and don't improperly succumb to weaknesses. You can underestimate your abilities, and instead, find your strengths and build your life. As you so progress, you won't have the constant pain. We don't live forever, so make the most of the time you have remaining. Keep in mind, you and others exist now. You could say to yourself, "I loved you so much that I will continue to live for you." Do not generate more pain for yourself; there is too much pain already, and life is too short already.

Charting Your Recovery

It is inevitable that with the variety of circumstances in life, improvement among people similarly will be varied.

The basic objective is to make some continual gain over time. Each person likely will have a different rate of recovery, that is, improvement in the direction of fuller functioning and adjustment over time. Family events, holidays, memories, financial stresses, personal challenges, health concerns, and interactions with others all serve to precipitate emotional responses that may support or hinder the rate of recovery.

As time progresses, events necessarily occur, and these ongoing events necessarily become part of your life, and you readjust as you deal with these events, and all the while, the date of the departed becomes more distant. In some respect, as your life proceeds, the expenditure/allocation of your life's energy/resources to grief could decrease over time.

POSSIBLE RATES OF RECOVERY CHARTS

Increasing Improvement

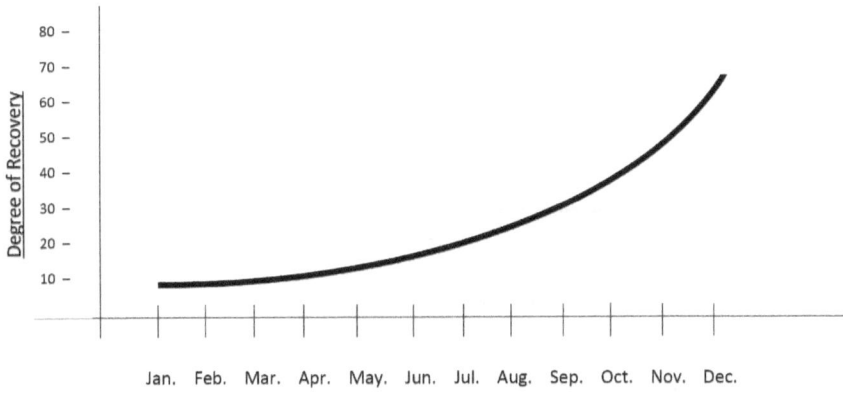

Continuous Improvement

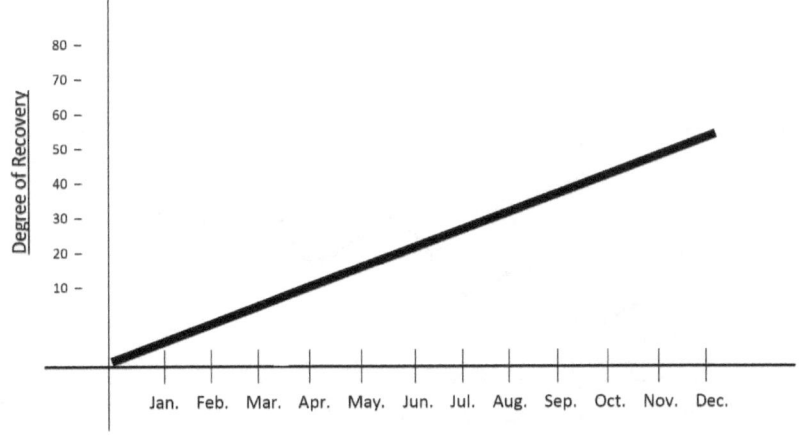

POSSIBLE RATES OF RECOVERY CHARTS

Delayed Improvement

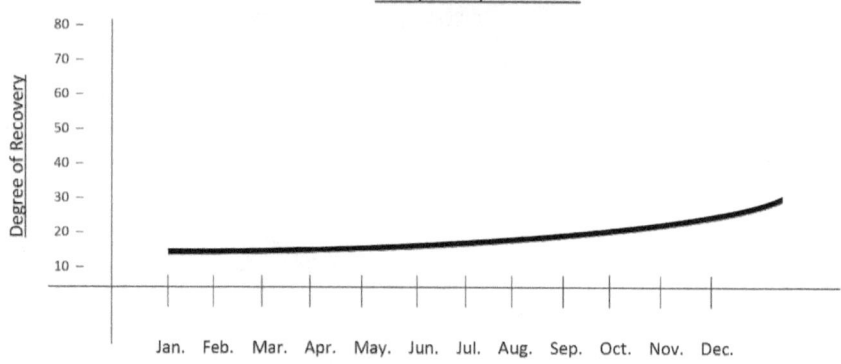

Variable Improvement with Progress

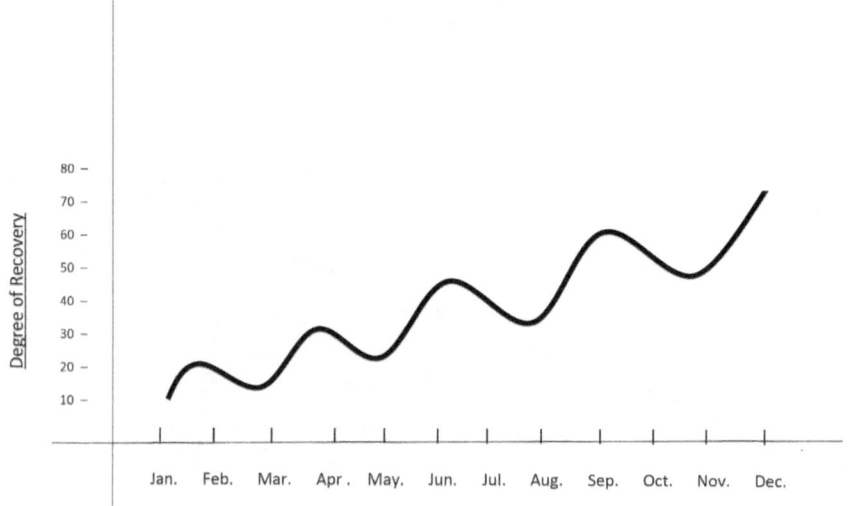

CHARTING YOUR RECOVERY

DEGREE OF RECOVERY OVER TIME

LIFE'S RESOUVOIR CONSUMED BY GRIEF OVER TIME

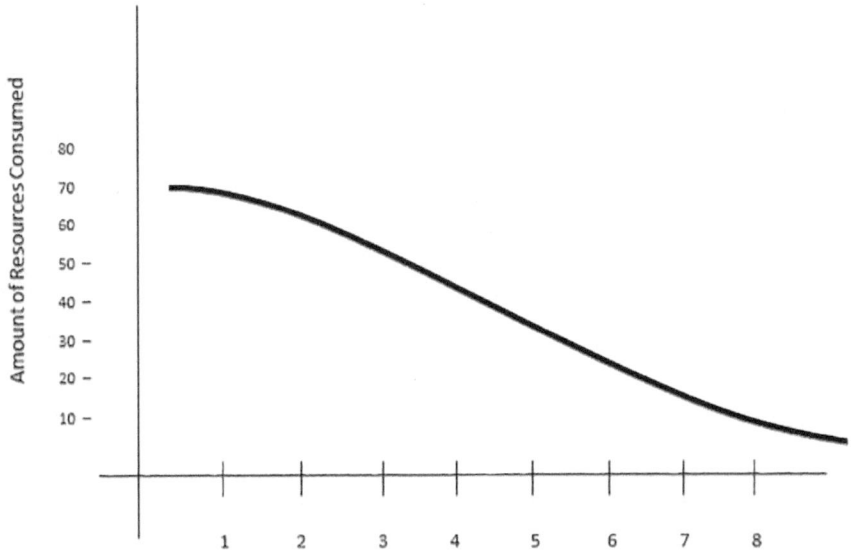

The time segments would vary with individuals, but in some cases might be, for example, six-month intervals.

While some suggest that a basic recovery time may be up to one-half the length of the relationship, we all have individual experiences and capabilities, and many progress sooner. Like many other conditions in life, time itself again may be the elixir of healing, as to some extent, this condition too will pass.

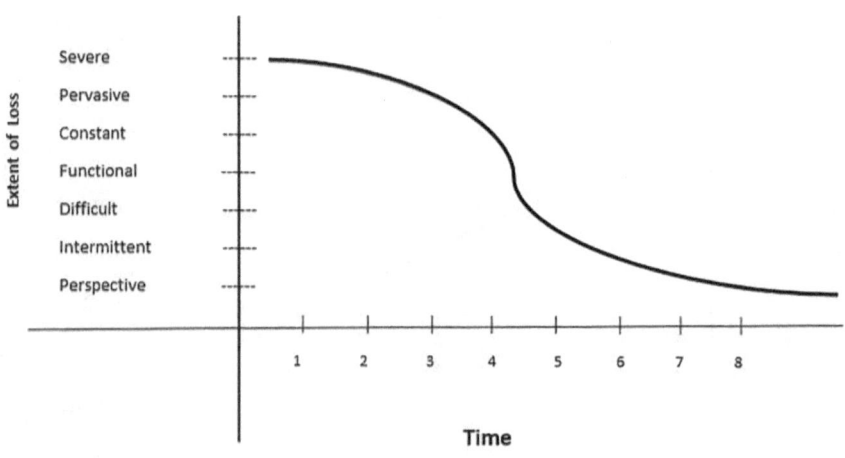

Some experiences suggest that the more intense the grief, the longer the course of recovery from the loss.

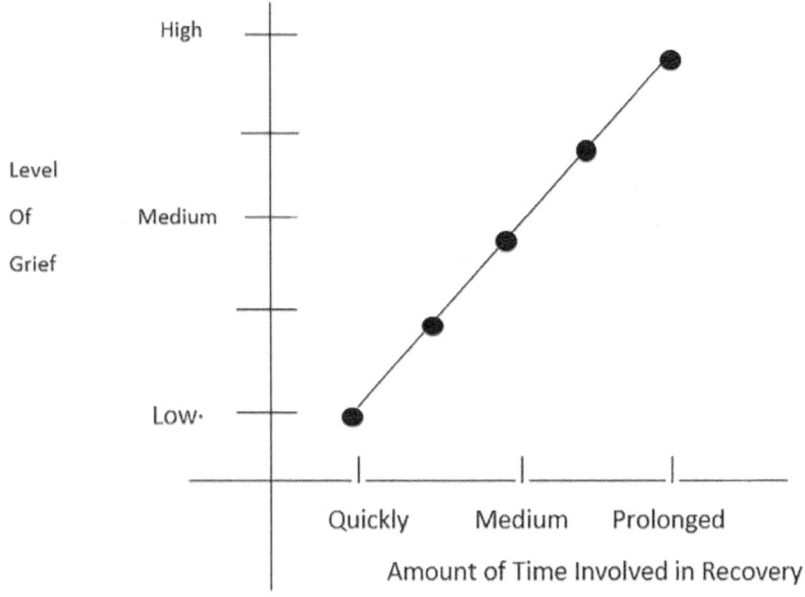

We all have a past—it becomes the foundation upon which we can build a new future, as the future is wide open to us now. The choice is clear—rather than not go on, first go on even without progressing, and then begin progressing, and live on to reach more perspective and return to a fuller life. The periods of pain become further and further apart, including all the I could haves, would haves, and/or should haves—intrusive thoughts. In between the pangs of grief, you live on, and over time, the pangs become less frequent and less severe. <u>You move from having bad days to having bad moments.</u> Eventually, the pains become memories, and those memories become a permanent honor you share for your deceased loved one. The pain may be like a Geiger counter, as even if there is always some residual ticking, it nevertheless becomes less intense. While there remain bumps in the road, you can keep moving forward.

For many, as your life enters its fourth quarter, your perspective necessarily begins to focus on preserving what remains of your life. As time proceeds, and as the amount of time remaining diminishes, its value per day increases. In some ways, your journey of recovery, from severe loss to less intense, becomes a lifetime experience of pain but also of greater understanding. It becomes more likely than not that you will begin to realize that after suffering such a loss, a year later, you improved somewhat, and then the following year, you became somewhat better, and with each passing year, you are not reliving the loss as severely. Your sense of belonging repositions itself from your past to your future. The next part of your life will be a better part of your life. Your victory is being alive to experience and appreciate each day.

Conclusion

IT TAKES TIME. In tragedy, we search to resurrect and rebuild. After all is considered, there really is no choice; you have to decide to work on wellness, to preserve your own gift of life, and to preserve the love and memory of your loved one. When stripped of all else, all you have is your optimism, and that is the seed from which you have the regrowth of a life. Just as nature abhors a vacuum, fill the void with your optimism for an emerging renaissance after darkness. Be the best you can be. Summon up the courage and faith to believe that better days are ahead and move yourself forward.

It is inevitable that we are going to join our lost loved one soon enough anyway, so live the remaining portion of your life to the fullest. We all go the way of all flesh. We all are going to be there before we know it, so why waste the time that you have left? We are going to be joining them sooner than we know anyway, so live life to the fullest now. There are many literary references regarding some initial feelings of wanting to join the lost loved one and not suffer pain of separation: Orpheus and Eurydice, Cleopatra and Marc Antony, Romeo and Juliet, but the reason they are tragedies is that they forsake all four:

- The gift of life you have been given:
- The richness of life you have yet to live;
- The love that the departed one had for you to be happy, and
- The responsibility you have to yourself and others not to multiply the loss, for example, as their surviving parent.

An example of this last factor was, while on a trip after losing my wife, all the children telephoned to make sure I was all right. Another example was my grandfather. He lost his first wife. He then remarried and had four lovely daughters, one of whom was my mother. However, I never knew until recently that he had a prior marriage. Letters I later found about his prior wife indicated that he had been very deeply affected and painfully hurt by that prior loss, but to me, his grandson, he thereafter had a fabulously full life of family, friends, activities, and a rewarding and respected career.

We have a future, we do get better, we have memories to cherish, and we have our life. Move out of the dark of despair and back into the light of life. There has been too much suffering already, and you can reach the broader perspective. They will continue to live on as long as they are remembered in the hearts of those who loved them. Even in grief, you may develop a deeper sense of life, of yourself, of others, and of appreciation for the gift of life.

About the Author

ERROL BERK studied at several universities, including Stanford University and the University of Southern California. He also studied in France and in England. He completed a Degree in Philosophy, and also had practiced Law for over forty years in litigation before his retirement. He lost his sister, and then two weeks later, on the date of his deceased brother's Yahrzeit, his wife also succumbed to illness. He has been examining bereavement considerably.

www.ingramcontent.com/pod-product-compliance
Lightning Source LLC
Chambersburg PA
CBHW021516120526
44766CB00007B/396